You Have Been Chosen for The Times

Awakening God's End Time Warriors

Keshia Freeland

You Have Been Chosen for The Times

Copyright © 2018 by Keshia Freeland

ISBN: 978-0-692-12526-7

Library of Congress Control Number: 2018906833

Printed in USA

DEDICATION

I dedicate this book first to the Father, Son, and Holy Spirit, my comforter and best friend. I thank God for the wisdom and ideas He gave me that birthed out this work. Secondly, to my dearest son, Isaiah, my supportive mom, Doris, and my dad, Ronald, for their love and support. Lastly, I dedicate this book to the entire upcoming generation of youth, that God is going to use to bring about transformation in this world.

TABLE OF CONTENTS

FORWORD

The word of God tells us that "many have been called but few are chosen". We have been called to do great things in this world in our allotted time but in order to be chosen you have to answer that call.

Esther was a queen chosen by the King but there was a greater call on her life that she had to answer. She was living in a time where her people/ Gods people were being persecuted because they were Jews. There came a day that their very lives were threatened to be taken away. Esther was called on by her uncle Mordecai to intercede for her people before the king.

Now there was a law at that time that said you could not approach the king unless you were summoned. Esther was now faced with the challenges that would defy natural laws but manifest the supernatural. Mordecai reminded her that she was "born into the kingdom for such a time as this". She decided "If I perish I perish" but I will go and see the King. She decided to answer a higher call on her life and as queen, intercede for her people to bring them to a place of freedom and victory.

Esther was chosen in her time from the foundation of the world for that great task and she fulfilled it. The people of God were free to fight for their lives and they lived in Victory.

Keisha Freeland is what I would call a modern-day Esther. Called of God to intercede for Gods people and bring them to a place of freedom and victory. To bring understanding of the times we live in and bring heaven to earth for Gods people. She has been Called and Chosen by God for the task. This book, *You Have Been Chosen for The Times* is the answer to that call.

"For God knew His people in advance, and He chose them to become like His Son, so that His Son would be the firstborn among many brothers and sisters. And having chosen them, He called them to come to Him. And having called them, He gave them right standing with himself. And having given them right standing, He gave them His glory."
Romans 8:29-30 NLT

Everyone born in this world has been handpicked by God for purpose. Life becomes fulfilled when you discover that purpose and begin to walk out that plan for your life. Knowing that you have been chosen for such a time as this is crucial; that alone gives you purpose and causes vision to come alive in you. Esther's identity wasn't revealed until it was time. You may feel like your purpose has been hidden but you are Gods best kept secret. God will be glorified in the earth and He has chosen you to shine through. Say yes to the call.

In Keshia Freeland's book *You Have Been Chosen for The Times* you will discover God's love and plan for humanity. And how that awesome plan plays out when you surrender your Life to Him. It's your season, it's your time! Enjoy discovering your journey as you read *You Have Been Chosen for The Times*.

Apostle Cynthia Brazelton,
Pastor of Victory Christian Ministries International, Suitland MD

ENDORSEMENTS

"It is a common saying that you do not judge a book by its cover but by the aroma of its contents. I am inhaling an aroma of glory about to be unleashed in the life of everyone that will read this book. This book will teach you how to fall like a grain of wheat to the ground and die, so that the glory buried within your destiny will be emerged. Drink the content of this book to show you the path that will enable you to break forth in your desired glory in Jesus."

Pastor Adebo Tomomewo
Founding pastor
Destiny Church For All Nations International
London and Washington D.C.

"I have read quite a few books in my life and I can truly say that I have not really come across any one as theologically pragmatic and riveting as this one. A seemingly incomprehensible spiritual and eschatological evolution is meticulously translated and simplified in the most intellectually permissible fashion ever. This book spontaneously ignites a Holy Anger within you!"

Joseph C Okechukwu
Actor, Director, CEO

"This book is a prophetic message to this generation and it will impact and transform any reader that dares to read it."

Dr. Denise Strothers
Pastor, Impact DMV

"Evangelist Keshia is a Woman of God that is completely sold out to the Lord. Her ministry is quite remarkable. In this book, you will discover that you, yes you, of all people have been chosen by God to make a difference."

Reverend Walter Timothy
Super Church
Ikeja, Lagos Nigeria

INTRODUCTION

Finding and fulfilling purpose is but the true satisfying fulfillment of life. God has invested too much in you and you are too important to Him. He is literally depending on you to bring the desired change in your community and nation. There is an invading of the supernatural force of God into the natural world. Underlying God's purposes and programs throughout all the ages, is to bring to a climax the full salvation of man. This is having the fallen man recreated or regenerated and growing up into perfection, in the image of Him who created Him. This is also having man attain the full measure of the stature of Christ, who is the express image of God.

In this realm of life, sickness, poverty, sorrow, and pains are no more, and death is completely abolished. This is Eden, this is paradise, and this is the Kingdom of God, where righteousness dwells. This realm is attainable now! I know you would not want to miss out on this. Consequently, the curtain is ready to be drawn up; all things are ready, and God is now set to unveil His Sons. To this end, God is restoring the Sonship message and the reality of the establishment of the Kingdom of God upon the earth. This Gospel seems to have been lost and put aside for over a century now. God is causing as many as are ordained or predestined for this, to enter into this realm of life. This is the fullness of the Spirit.

In this book, the author, in prophetic undertones, unravels the mystery of the coming salvation by the Elect and Chosen ones, who are the manifestation of the Sons of God at this close of the church age, to the intent that those whom God apprehends may be fully apprehended and persuaded to know the exceeding riches of His grace towards us. These are those whom God has chosen in love before the foundation of the world to the praise of His glory and to know the exceeding greatness of His power that is available to us, in us and through us, whom He has chosen to display the manifold or multi-dimensional wisdom of God, unto the principalities and powers by the Church in this age and that which is to come. This book is very timely. Be warned! This book is revolutionary. It will upturn your conventional, religious worldview and beliefs and set you ablaze on fire with holy desire to lay hold of the fullness of God in Christ. Above all, it promises to be a blessing to all who read it and give heed to the words of this prophecy.

CHAPTER ONE
THE GREATEST LOVE STORY EVER TOLD

THE FALL

God created man for His glory, to have fellowship and intimacy with Him, like a union between a man and wife, but man lost precious and supernatural relationship was short lived as a result of man's disobedience to instruction.

The absence of light, births darkness

In Genesis 3:1-3 it says *"Now the serpent was craftier than any of the wild animals the LORD God had made. He said to the woman, "Did God really say, 'You must not eat from any tree in the garden'?" 2 The woman said to the serpent, "We may eat fruit from the trees in the garden, 3 but God did say, 'You must not eat fruit from the tree that is in the middle of the garden, and you must not touch it, or you will die.'"*

This disobedience drove man out of the light and glory of God where man was in charge, into the realm of darkness level where man was at the mercies of the devil.

WHY HE DIED

Right from the day of separation of man from his creator, God was searching for ways to reunite and reconcile man back to Himself, and as long as man was under sin, he was off the radar of God because the eyes of God are too holy to behold sin.

Man, on the other hand, were also struggling to redeem and get close to God because he was tired of living at the mercies of the devil. To achieve this, man sacrificed bulls, sheep, birds and all kinds of animals to atone for his sins. (Leviticus 1:1-7)

But you see, the best this sacrifice could do was cover man sins. It's like covering a portion of a white cloth stained with ink, no matter the coverage, it does not remove the ink stain on the white cloth, because when the clothe is exposed, the ink stain will still be visible.

This was the same faith of man based on the atonement of sins using animals. So, man was relying on this avenue, but he was still in enmity and condemnation with God. To crown it all, at Mt. Sinai, the Israelis signed up for a law-based covenant where God's blessing and redemption with them would be based on their faithfulness to keeping the law according to Exodus 19:8-25 and Exodus 20:1-21.

THE PURPOSE OF THE LAW

Joyce Meyer once said that when the purpose of a thing is not known, then abuse is inevitable. Many Christians are not aware of the purpose of the law. The question is why was the law (Mosaic) given? Apostle Tony Brazelton said this, *"We can't appreciate the work of Jesus on the Cross if we don't know who we were under the law in the eyes of the Lord."*

This ignorance has made lot of Christians to believe that the law can make them perfect in Gods eyes, or by keeping the law, they can please God and receive salvation. The law cannot save you, the law cannot make you perfect, either will you be keeping the law or receiving the salvation of God. Romans 3:20-26 says, *"Therefore, by the deeds of the law there shall no flesh be justified in His sight: for by the law is the knowledge of sin. But now the righteousness of God without the law is manifested, being witnessed by the law and the prophets; Even the righteousness of God which is by faith of Jesus Christ unto all and upon all them that believe: for there is no difference: For all have sinned, and come short of the glory of God; Being justified freely by His grace through the redemption that is in Christ Jesus: Whom God hath set forth to be a propitiation through faith in His Blood, to declare His righteousness for the remission of sins that are past, through the forbearance of God; To declare, I say, at this time His righteousness: that He might be just, and the justifier of Him which believeth in Jesus."*

From the above scripture the only way to be in right standing with God, is not by your works, but by accepting the work of Jesus at the Cross and making Him master over your life.

So, the purpose of the law was to convict man of sin, to bring man to a point where he realizes that he needs God totally, that he cannot please God by his work, but rather depend on the mercies and grace of God, to reveal Jesus, and point man to the cross. (Luke 24:44-45, Romans 3:20)

The greater question now is; was man able to fulfill the law? NO. Only Jesus could fulfill the law and redeem man from sin and condemnation and restore man to God. At the cross Jesus said, *"It is finished."* He took our sins and died for the world according to Second Corinthians 5:21. He fulfilled the law and bought us redemption.

At His death on the Cross, righteousness was imputed into man, and man exchanged his sin and mortality with the righteousness and divinity of Christ. All we are expected to do to receive this priceless gift is to believe and accept Jesus Christ. (Romans 3:21-26) What a glorious and eternal victory for man!

We are no longer under the law, for we have been redeemed from the law and all of the curses it brings; sin has no dominion over us. Romans 6:14 says, *"For sin shall not have dominion over you: for ye are not under the law, but under grace. Only the death of Jesus could achieve this."*

Because of Christs death, we were not only reconciled to God but rather, we were placed in a better relationship with God. Man became a carrier of the presence of God in the person of Jesus, unlike Adam and Eve who only received the presence of God at a certain time of the day. We have a deeper romance and intimacy with God through Jesus Christ. We have become little Gods in Gods eyes. (Psalm 82:6) Hallelujah!

WE ARE BEING CALLED TO REINTRODUCE JESUS BACK TO THIS GENERATION

The Holy Scriptures allude to the fact that God Himself is Love. His essence, character and being is Love. In other words, He isn't the quintessence. He is Love. In First Corinthians 13, the Bible noted that *"if we speak in the tongues of men and Angels and perform all kinds spiritual activities but have no Love, then we're no better than a noisy drum (paraphrased)."*

It actually implies that no matter how good the works of our hands may be; or how strictly we observe sundry religious rights, if we do all that without an assurance that the King of Glory Himself (who is Love) lives in us, we're simply wasting our time.

By sending His "Only Begotten Son" for the redemption of mankind, God clearly demonstrated this love essence which He embodies in its totality. It is at best the purest and most undiluted kind of love, laced with sacrificial elements on all sides. It is inconvenient; It is extravagant; It is both incontrovertible and all encompassing. It is the greatest kind of love. No wonder love is so tedious and terrifying without the God who in Himself is Love.

So, when the bible says *"...for God so loved the world,"* it refers to the far reaching and immeasurable magnitude of His love for a world that was completely lost in sin and disobedience.

So, loved doesn't just speak to the magnitude, it also speaks to the unconditionality of this unique love. Often times as human beings, we measure love by how much commensurate actions the potential recipients may have provoked to deserve or not deserve our show of love.

And even when we show love, we often, almost unconsciously wait around for reciprocation, the absence of which could greatly inhibit our capacity to sustain the habit of love. It's an innate and intrinsic human disposition to attach pre-and post-conditions to love and loving.

The bible says that the heart of man is inherently wicked, that is why the human nature naturally abhors sacrificial and unconditional love. In other words, a natural man can never love unconditionally.

But a man filled with the Holy Ghost would spontaneously exhibit in greater measures, the characteristics of unconditional love because the Holy Spirit of God is an embodiment of the God who in Himself is Love. So, when He lives in us, loving becomes a natural and spontaneous way of life.

To better appreciate what God did in sending His "Only Begotten Son," we need to first of all understand and appreciate the fact that Jesus was "The Only Son" that is on record as "Begotten" by God. In other words, the only son that came directly out of His loins. Imagine how emotionally and psychologically attached a father would naturally be to his only son.

As a father, you'd be incredibly obsessed with that son; You'd want to have him around you every minute of the day; You wouldn't want anything whatsoever to hurt him; That child becomes your heartbeat, your weakest point!

Imagine having to sacrifice a son like that knowing he'd go through some of the most horrifying and dehumanizing experiences ever known to mankind. The only human semblance of this action that comes to mind is Abraham and Isaac.

I believe that Abraham's prophetic exercise with his son had God's hands tied to the extent that in the fullness of time, even if mankind is found to be too far away from God, He'd still send His son, because father Abraham had pre-qualified us and that pre-qualification became a covenant in which God could not renege. It showed that father Abraham's version of humanity had learned sacrificial love from Abba Father and deserved a reciprocation whenever the need arose.

God is an incredible covenant keeper. He functions better in the realms of covenant. Love and loving is a covenant. The Holy Spirit is the High priest of that covenant. Because God has unleashed unconditional love on us, He expects us to unleash on one another without limitations.

If we were deserving of it when He unleashed it, we'd be having a big mouth to contend or pick and choose. Unfortunately, we were not deserving of it so unleashing on one another becomes a command. And we desperately need the Holy Spirit to obey God in that regard.

If we put the past, the present and the future together, we wouldn't come any close to a Love greater than this- that God gave His "Only Begotten Son" to redeem mankind from the shackles of eternal death, and He did it happily, ungrudgingly and without regrets.

CHAPTER TWO
THE DAY I WAS CHOSEN

I knew the day I was chosen by God was the day I discovered that everything surrounding my life was about to change drastically. What I thought I knew about life was totally wrong and the day I said yes to Jesus was the day I said yes to life.

I did not grow up in church at all, so I knew what I was experiencing, or feeling was not normal for a girl growing up in a kind of urban community were the norms are partying, drugs, premarital sex, and just living for the moment without any sense of purpose. So, coming into the reality that the God that created the whole world would want and be interested in a girl like me was unfathomable and mind blowing to me.

And till this day, it is so hard for me to wrap my natural mind around God, Himself the Master Strategist, the Completer of everything, the All Wise One who had in His mind to choose me before the foundation of the earth, to carry His glorious gospel into all the world despite my imperfections. This indeed is my greatest asset knowing that He chose me.

What I thought I knew about life was totally wrong and the day I said yes to Jesus was the day I said yes to life

Did you know you were chosen by God before the foundation of the world? He chose you because He loves you. When you know you have been chosen it makes you feel special. The Apostle Paul used the word elect to refer to being chosen.

Do you know what it means to be the elect of God? It means, you are handpicked by God. Once you fully understand what Paul was saying, you will find it easy to walk in your true identity in Christ. You will begin to think consciously, *"I am chosen by God. Of course, He will heal me. Of course, He will give me victory over any obstacles and challenges I come across in this life."*

Peter said to the "elect exiles" that is, to Christians scattered throughout the Roman Empire *"You are a chosen race, a royal priesthood, a holy nation, a people for His own possession"* (1 Peter 2:9). He meant it as an enormous encouragement for a tiny, beleaguered, persecuted minority in a vast sea of unbelief and growing hostility.

The adversaries may seem powerful, numerous, dangerous and dominant. But look again! You are God's chosen ones!

WHAT DOES GOD CHOOSING YOU SIGNIFY?

1. **Your faith is not the basis of God's choosing**
   This means that your faith is a way more wonderful than any of the seven wonders of the world. Jesus said, *"You did not choose me, but I chose you"* (John 15:16). And there was a deeper choosing going on here than just the selection of the Twelve. We know this because Judas was part of the Twelve, and he was not "chosen." Jesus said, *"I am not speaking of all of you; I know whom I have chosen. But the Scripture will be fulfilled, 'He who ate My bread has lifted his heel against Me'"* (John 13:18).

Your roots, as a child of God, are in eternity — in the infinite mind and heart of God!

If you have come to Jesus, the wonder is that you already belonged to the Father, and the Father gave you to Jesus. You were not chosen because you came; you came because you were chosen. That's what Jesus said: *"All that the Father gives me will come to me. Yours they were, and You gave them to Me"* (John 6:37; 17:6). If you have believed on Jesus, the wonder is that you were first appointed to eternal life. You weren't appointed because you believed; you believed because you were appointed.

When the Gentiles heard that the gospel included them, *"they began rejoicing and glorifying the Word of the Lord, and as many as were appointed to eternal life believed"* (Acts 13:48). Revel in the wonder that you are a Christian because God chose you to be one. Your roots, as a child of God, are in eternity - in the infinite mind and heart of God. Your faith, and all its fruits, are God's eternal gift.

2. **The basis of God choosing you is not in you, but in grace**
Take God's Old Testament people Israel, for example. Why did God set His favor on Israel above all the peoples of the earth? What was the basis of God's calling them "My Chosen" in Isaiah 45:4? Here's Moses's answer:

The Lord your God has chosen you to be a people for His treasured possession, out of all the peoples who are on the face of the earth. It was not because you were more in number than any other people that the Lord set His love on you and chose you, for you were the fewest of all peoples, but it is because the Lord loves you and is keeping the oath that He swore to your fathers.

Deuteronomy 7:6–8

This is amazing: "The Lord set His love on you and chose you because the Lord loves you." He loves you because He loves you! That's the deepest and ultimate basis of God choosing Israel.

Paul underlines the wonder. Why was Jacob, the father of the nation of Israel, chosen over his twin brother Esau? Paul answers in Romans 9:11-12:

"Though they were not yet born, and had done nothing either good or bad in order that God's purpose to choose might continue, not because of works but because of Him who calls their mother was told, 'The older will serve the younger'"

And the principle holds today. Paul would say, *"So too at the present time there is a remnant, chosen by grace"* (Romans 11:5). So, it is with every true Christian. Behind our believing, behind our coming to Jesus, is grace alone. There is no ground for our being chosen beneath the all-wise and incomprehensible love of God. Oh, the vastness of the repercussions of this unfathomable truth!

13

3. **Since our faith and obedience is owing to God's choice of us, we can know we are chosen**

It is a wonder that God's unfathomable, eternal choice of who will be His children can be known by those He chose. Paul said that He knew the Thessalonian believers were God's chosen ones. *"We know, brothers loved by God, that He has chosen you."* (1 Thessalonians 1:4).

Only God's eternal resolve to save His chosen people can explain the miracle of faith that receives the Word of the Gospel with joy in the midst of affliction. This is the work of God, and God does this saving work for His chosen ones. If it has happened to you, you may know that you are chosen. Let the wonder of this sink in. Your faith is not a witness to any prior power in you. It is a witness to God's choosing you. It is not a testimony to something so small as self-determination. It is a testimony to the same power that created the universe. God chose to raise you from the dead (Ephesians 2:5).

4. **Being chosen by God means, no charge against you can affect you**

The multiplied wonders of God's choosing a people, include the unfathomable fact that God sent His Son into the world to cancel all the debts of His chosen ones to nullify every condemning accusation against them, and to give them a righteous standing in the court of heaven.

If God is for us, who can be against us? He who did not spare his own Son but gave him up for us all, how will he

not also with him graciously give us all things? Who shall
bring any charge against God's chosen ones? It is God
who justifies. Who is to condemn? Christ Jesus is the one
who died more than that, who was raised who is at the
right hand of God, who indeed is interceding for us.
Romans 8:31–34

Your faith in Jesus is a wonder more
wonderful than any of the seven wonders
of the world

The reason no charge can stick to God's chosen ones is that
God "gave [His Son] up for us," and it necessarily follows
that God will "graciously give us all things."

The wonder is not only that there is "no condemnation," but
that this was all planned in eternity to be Omnipotent
successful. He did not do this great work like a fisherman
throwing a net to see who might swim into it. We did not just
happen to swim into God's salvation. This was planned and
performed with a special view of us, the chosen ones.

5. **Being chosen by God is designed to secure for us the**
   sweetness of humility
   The more we consider being chosen, the more the wonder of
   it grows. And Paul tells us to *consider* it. The reason he
   wants us to think about being chosen, is that it will make us
   humble. Here's the passage that makes this point. He starts
   by telling us to consider our "calling," because this calling
   from death to life is the way we experience in *time* the choice

He made in *eternity*. Then he mentions three times our being chosen.

Consider your calling, brothers: not many of you were wise according to worldly standards, not many were powerful, not many were of noble birth. But God chose what is foolish in the world to shame the wise; God chose what is weak in the world to shame the strong; God chose what is low and despised in the world, even things that are not, to bring to nothing things that are, so that no human being might boast in the presence of God. 1 Corinthians 1:26–29

Do you see the point? God is free to choose who will become a Christian. And in His freedom, He explodes expectations of who is "special." Just when we think we may have Him figured out in His choosing, we see He has gone another way. Paul doesn't leave us to guess what the point is. It is this: *"so that no human being might boast in the presence of God."* God's choosing is designed to remove our boasting. Any group, or any person, who boasts that there is something in them that justifies God's choosing them, has not experienced what the choosing is for. It is for the annihilation of self as the basis of God's favor. We did nothing absolutely nothing to qualify for being chosen.

6. **Being chosen by God means being destined for the everlasting, all-satisfying praise of the infinitely beautiful God**

The wonder is that the ultimate aim of being chosen is the ultimate joy of being satisfied. And the wonder deepens as we realize that we human beings were designed to find our fullest satisfaction, not in front of a mirror, but in front of God. We were made to be mirrors, not see mirrors. Mirrors with eyes. And the joy of seeing all-satisfying Beauty was meant to find its consummation in the reflection of that beauty to God and man in praise.

This is what Paul says in Ephesians 1:4–6. God *"chose us"* and *"predestined us . . . to the praise of the glory of His grace."*

7. **Being chosen by God means that God will use all necessary means to bring you to this eternal glory**
The wonder of being chosen includes the wonder that God has chosen to bring us home. Glory is not immediate and not automatic.

> Through many dangers, toils, and snares,
> I have already come, and
> 'is grace that brought me safe thus far,
> And grace will lead me home.

We do not travel from new birth to new earth without the trials of a traveler. And if God had not chosen for us to be helped by many fellow travelers, we would not make it. That's why Paul says:

> *"Therefore I endure everything for the sake of the chosen ones, that they also may obtain the salvation that is in Christ Jesus with eternal glory."*
> 2 Timothy 2:10

Paul himself was a God-chosen means of saving the chosen ones. So are you. You are one. And you need others. For God's chosen ones, the means are necessary, and they are certain. For God has chosen them as surely as He has chosen you.

8. **Being chosen by God means that God shapes history and suspends protocols on your behalf**

This wonder may be too much for us to comprehend, but here it is: *"If those days had not been cut short, no human being would be saved. But for the sake of the chosen ones those days will be cut short."* (Matthew 24:22)

We were designed to find our fullest satisfaction not in front of a mirror, but in front of God

---

The flow of history will be altered. For the sake of the chosen ones. Protocols will be suspended for you. The world of unbelievers, who reject God and His Son, have no idea how the world is run. They do not know what true significance is.

9. **Finally, being chosen by God means He will gather us when He comes and give us justice**

The wonder of vindication is coming. It may be that in this life the chosen ones were treated just like Jesus a stone which the builders rejected.

But in God's sight that stone was "chosen and precious" (1 Peter 2:4, 6). And that very stone became the cornerstone of

18

the Kingdom of God (1 Peter 2:6–8). He rose from the dead. There was a glorious vindication. I am handpicked by God, and I have been set apart for him. God spoke through the prophet Jeremiah saying, before I formed you in the womb, I knew you, before you were born I sanctified you. (Jeremiah 1:5)

Protocols are broken when you have been chosen for the times

Knowing this gives you great confidence that God is going to see you through any situation in your life. So, no matter what you are experiencing today whether it be past, present or future. You are constantly comforted that God is with you and will bring you out of it.

Chosen means to be selected or marked for favor or special privileges; selected from or preferred above others; the chosen few or remnant; having been selected by God.

The synonyms for chosen are selected, favored, picked, appointed, and elected. The Greek word for chosen is "eklektos" meaning chosen, elect, select, chosen out by God for the rendering of a special service to Him. After doing intense research and study on the definition and meaning of chosen, it gave me a great desire to write this book to empower and inspire you.

I remember the event leading up to the most important decision I will make in my life as a human being, this was the day I gave my life to Jesus Christ, the day Grace found me, the day I was chosen to be a witness and a testimony of the message of the cross, the day I died to myself.

Growing up as a teen in an environment and a country where my fellow teenagers were busy partying, taking drugs, selling their body for fun, staying out late at night at clubs, this was the social norms of the day at that time, but there was something calling me from the inside, there was a force drawing me out from such a lifestyle, I felt destiny calling my name. Jesus was setting me apart like a special vessel for an ultimate assignment.

Because of my withdrawal and refusal not to get entangled into such a lifestyle, I was considered a weird and very religious person, due to my convictions and commitment to serve God. But you see, because I said yes to God, my yes created a change in my environment among my friends, and today many of them are born again and on fire for the Lord, some are even pastors and ministers doing great exploits for the Lord, simply because a fifteen-year-old teenager, said yes to Jesus.

I remember being invaded by the God of Heaven to decide not only to give my life to Him as personal Savior but to make Him Master over all the affairs of my life. I remember saying to myself someday *"What is it?"* why am I feeling the weight of something upon me that is not of this world. There were days I would lock myself up in my closest and ask God, *'What do you want from me?'* and I remember in that moment, I would always feel the tangible presence of His love filling me up and wrapping me up like a blanket.

It was as though my whole being was saturated with liquid fire that could consume anything that came in its way and my way, like a wall around me. So, the heaviness of His hand upon my life, at that very moment, gave me a peace that He was there, and He was ready to spend time sharing His heart, not only for my destiny, but for the destiny of many others that He was sending me to release His relentless and uncontrollable love.

THE RESTRAINING POWER OF GOD

There is a power that God gave His elect to restrain Satan's ability to rule over them. I have chosen to call this power "the restraining power." This power is the power of the Holy Spirit that intervenes on three levels and restrains Satan's ability to exercise his power according to his will.

When we are born again, our bodies become the temple of the Holy Spirit. (1 Corinthians 3:16) The Holy Spirit indwells us and empowers us to resist Satan's devices. It is our responsibility to use this "restraining power" to resist the works of the flesh. Romans 8:13 says, *"For if you live according to the flesh you will die; but if by the Spirit you put to death the deeds of the body, you will live."*

The works of the flesh (Galatians 5 and Colossians 3) are those areas through which Satan promotes temptation and entices us. We are told to resist him.

In First Peter 5:8-9 the Bible says, *"Be sober, be vigilant; because your adversary the devil walks about like a roaring lion, seeking whom he may devour. Resist him, steadfast in the faith, knowing that the same sufferings are experienced by your brotherhood in the world."*

The Bible says in James 4:7, *"Therefore submit to God. Resist the devil and he will flee from you."* We have a promise from God that Satan will flee from us if we will resist him. We must, however, submit to the rule of the Holy Spirit who indwells us. If we do this, then we are empowered by the Spirit, and we can resist Satan effectively.

This is the first level of the use of the restraining power. It is for personal use by which Satan is restrained from his ability to rule over the believer. If we use the power that we have been given, then we will live the victorious overcoming life. This is the Master's promise to His people as He said in Luke 10:19, *"Behold, I give you the authority to trample on serpents and scorpions, and over all the power of the enemy, and nothing shall by any means hurt you."*

CHAPTER THREE
THE DAY I DIED

Life is a product of death, just as the seed of a plant cannot manifest its potential as a tree until it enters the soil and decays (dies), so it is with human life. I never knew what I was embarking on and the journey I was about to take when deciding to give my life and desires over to Jesus Christ, I did not know it was going to be this awesome and life-transforming.

Everybody comes to a point in their life when they have to die. Yes, I said die. But the question is, die to what? Die to self, die to lust, die to flesh, die to everything that exalteth itself above God in our lives? The Bible says in John 12: 24, *"Verily, I say unto you, except a grain of wheat falls into the ground and die, it abided alone, but if it dies, if bringeth forth much fruit."*

Death is an important factor of life. For a man to truly live his dreams, and goals, he undergoes a certain kind of death experience to get rid of any form of distractions or barricade to the fulfillment of the dreams in his heart.

Life in Christ is a product of death

Every successful and world changers personality in different areas of life, be it ministry, science, literature, economy, art, entertainment, anything, are men and women who have decided to die to certain areas of their life. For you to start living, you must first die, because death comes before truly living.

People like my Pastors, Apostle Tony and Cynthia Brazelton, Joyce Meyer, Kathryn Kuhlman, Cindy Trimm, Bill Gates, Nelson Mandela, Myles Munroe, Mother Theresa, the Patriarch Abraham, and many other great men and women that have left generational impact on the world and are still impacting the world, all died to certain attributes in their life, so as to fulfill Gods perfect and divine will for their lives.

Some of them died to greed, the lust of the flesh, their own will, career, family and some relationships. So, you see, the death experience is a necessity to true existence in Christ. Jesus Christ also died for Him to fully fulfill His purpose on earth, before Jesus died, He was limited by time and distance, as a result He could not be in two places at the same time.

But after His death, He became limitless of time and place, He could be in India and be in Washington at the same time, His death unleashed a multiplier effect in the world. How? He reproduced Himself in everyone that accepted Him, this was why the princes of this world said in First Corinthians 2:7-8:

But we speak the wisdom of God in a mystery, even the hidden wisdom, which God ordained before the world unto our glory, for which none of the princes of this world knew; for had they known it, they would not have crucified the lord of glory.

Can you see that even the devil knew the power of Christ death? He knew what the death of Jesus would bring to the world and he was regretting the fact that God used him to kill Jesus, because Jesus' death broke the limitation of time and distance. Before His death, Jesus as a person in a body, was only able to communicate to one person at a time, but after His death, the Bible said the veil was torn and the partition was lifted, and the earth did quake, and the rocks rent. (Matthew 27:50-51)

Jesus was no longer in one body but rather He was reproduced and lives on the inside of everyone that accepts Him as their Lord and Savior, working miracles and transforming life. That is the power of death, that is the power of dying to self and surrendering ones will to the Will of the almighty God. Jesus said in Luke 22:42, *"Father, if You are willing, take this cup from Me; yet not My Will, but Yours be done."*

So, because Jesus died to His own Will and surrendered to the Will of God, He was exalted and given a Name above every other name, that at the mention of His Name, every knee must bow, and every tongue confess that He (Christ) is the Lord. (Philippians 2:10-11, Romans 14:11).

Beloved, whenever we go into a death experience like Jesus did with God in any area of our lives that is not in alignment with the Word, or whenever we decide to die to our will and surrender to the Supreme Will of God for our life, it unleashes the greatness and gifting in us because of His presence in our life, for the point of discovery of destiny begins at the point of death in Christ.

The scriptures say in First John 4: 17:

"And we have seen and do testify that the Father sent the Son to be the Savior of the world. Whosoever shall confess that Jesus is the Son of God, God dwelleth in him, and he in God. And we have known and believed the love that God hath to us. God is love; and he that dwelleth in love dwelleth in God, and God in him. Herein is

our love made perfect, that we may have boldness in the day of judgment: because as he is, so are we in this world."

I pray that the spirit of obedience to Gods Will and calling in your life come upon you. Amen.

I remember that day I met with Jesus, it was an unforgettable encounter, of which I am yet to recover from.

That day, I died to myself, my will and my desires, I surrendered my life to Him and decided to live His Will for my life, right from that day a supernatural woman was unleashed from the inside of me, it was like I have been living like a sheep whereas on the inside I was a lion, a champion, a victor, and a transformer.

I saw myself like clay, whereas I was a diamond to be treasured, a rare gift to the world. And right from that day till present I have experienced the miraculous. That death experience opens my eyes to the gift and calling of God in my life, things I would not have done in my natural self but due to the supernatural in me, I am doing them today.

The point of destiny discovery begins at death in Christ

His death for me and my death to His will for me brought me to this new dimension of living. It is urgent that we surrender all for the kingdom of God and lay down our lives so that someone else will live. Jesus is our perfect example because He laid down His life so the whole world could be saved and redeemed to God. (Luke 9:23-26)

CHAPTER FOUR
LIFE FROM THE UNSEEN

We are first and foremost a spirit living in a natural body learning to see, hear and access the spirit realm and its principles. Learning to live life through the eyes of the spirit is transforming and freeing.

Living from the unseen reveals that we can live life through the eyes of the Spirit and with an awareness of the spiritual realities and principals that affect our everyday lives. This is a book that shares insights on how to obtain a transformed life through the renewing of the mind through the Word of God.

Living every day in the realms of the supernatural means to draw your strength for daily living from God. In Psalms 84:2 the Scripture says, *"My soul longest, yea, even fainted for the courts of the Lord: my heart and my flesh cry out for the Living God."*

David did not mince words in relaying his heartfelt and fanatically emotional attachment to the presence of the Highest God. "Longest" and "Fainted" are words you'd easily hear from a true Lover who is helplessly in love with his Beloved. He even took it further by saying *"...his heart and his flesh cries out..."* Now if that doesn't connote a passionate emotional engagement, I don't know what does.

When a man is truly in love with a woman, he literally loses his mind. His entire emotional energy is spontaneously directed at that woman and he suddenly becomes both protective of her and jealous over her. Every minute he gets to spend with her is like a lifetime in heaven. Every second she's away from him is like eternity in misery.

It's not just an incredible magnetic attachment, it's an unbreakable emotional interdependency. Here we mirror the reactions of just one party- David. When we hear God's side of the love affair, we hear things like *"I am a jealous God...thou shall not do this, or do that, or share My this or My that with anybody!"* It's a serious affair!

To live solely off the supernatural simply means you've been totally and completely sold out. Your sustenance and inspiration come from that realm. Your essence and livelihood come from there.

You breathe, speak and live the supernatural. The supernatural literally oozes out of you; It permeates your environment; It announces your presence and distinguishes you in the realms of the natural. The supernatural becomes you!

Unlike the "seen" realm, the "unseen" realm is characterized by its huge potentials for unpredictability. John 3:8 says *"The wind blew where it listed, and thou hear the sound thereof, but canst not tell whence it cometh, and whither it goeth: so is everyone that is born of the Spirit."* So, if you're born of the Spirit you'll have to live by the Spirit.

And if you live by the Spirit, you're unpredictable, you're more of a doer not a talker, you're an incredible influencer, you're a history maker, you're a pioneer of transformational and revolutionary ideologies, you're a world changer! People will know you more by their encounter with your exploits.

The fruits of the Spirit of God which dwell in you shall evidently distinguish you. As the saying goes, "it is the supernatural that controls the natural". Whatever happens in our material world is decided, programmed and projected from the realms of the "unseen"- be it positive or negative.

Living from a positive, divine "unseen" world means living above the mundanities and limitations of a material world; it means operating in the absoluteness of the supernatural dimensions of sacred divinity.

The Superpower of God, placed on our natural abilities like speaking, produces a portal (doorway) for the Supernatural to be released in whatever atmosphere we find ourselves. It is vital that we come into full synchronization with the Father in this very day.

It's never too late to start again. When the person of the Holy Spirit is directing your steps, you can regain years in just a moment. Divine moments with God interrupts the natural course of events and propels you into the supernatural where all things are possible. We must be Governed by the eternal perspective everyday of our lives. It should consume and overwhelm us then Propel us into full action!

Faith was given to you for someone else! The more you Release Faith; The more your Faith Will Increase. Eyes have not seen, nor has it entered the heart of man, the things that are about to take place upon Planet Earth.

You have entered the Glory Zone where time doesn't matter and there are endless possibilities with no limitations or measurements.

We need the Glory of God for the next Season of Church History, the End Times.

You were given the responsibility to help define the nature of the world that we live in. This reveals the heart of God in such a beautiful way. God did not create us to be robots. We were made in HIS image as co-laborers, working with HIM to demonstrate His goodness over all that He made.

The crown of God's creation was a new creature that can sound the heartbeat of its Creator. We reflect The Father's own relational richness. The human family is to join the Father in the ongoing work of Creation and taking the Gospel of Jesus Christ into all the Nations of the World!

The Cross of Jesus restored us back to the Father's Purpose for us in His Original Intent! The story of humanity's sin begins with a tree and ends on a tree: first, the tree of the knowledge of good and evil; and finally, the cross on which Jesus dies. The first tree offers fruit that leads to death, but the second offers a death that leads to eternal life. The day you discover HIM you discover your Purpose. The day you give your life to HIM you start the Journey to fulfill the fullness of true sonship.

We get used to Religious Practices that keep us in a deep Sleep and a life of settlement and defeat. The life of Purpose is full of adventures and Encounters with the Father, Son, and Holy Spirit and access to the Heavenly Realms!

Many fail to realize that what is needed in this pursuit of more is an abandonment to God that attracts something that cannot be explained, controlled, or understood. We must encounter one who is bigger than we are in every possible way until He leaves a mark. He is purpose and you become PURPOSE the day you discover Him. Everything that you know as life or everything that you are used to suddenly changes. You're a critical lifeline to many who are dead, devastated, hurt, confused, hopeless, depressed and Blind.

We must Wake up and Awaken to the Reality that we were born in the Middle of a War Zone and we must think with a Military Mind Set! Because we are called to train this Generation to be strong, Anointed and equipped Soldiers.

THE UNSEEN REALM

The reason you must come to Reality with your purpose is, you were born in the Middle of a War Zone between the Seen and the Unseen Realm. You must know Jesus as your Lord and King and Satan as your Enemy because our enemy has a well-orchestrated kingdom, as you can see by the chaos and confusion in the world. But the Good News is that Jesus Christs Kingdom shall never come to an end because it is an everlasting Kingdom, the Bible states that even the government shall rest upon His shoulders. Beloved your very prayers of Intercession alter History by releasing legions of Angels into the Earth. If we grasp this truth, we would pray with intensity, and we would pray constantly.

The conflict in the world is in the Unseen Realm and some of us are fighting a losing battle with fleshly Weapons. Second Corinthians 10:4 say, *"For the Weapons of our Warfare are not carnal, but mighty through God to the pulling down of strongholds."*

When I look at the cities of the United States, I see Christians sleepwalking through their daily affairs in life and no one seems to understand that we have shifted into a State of Urgency! We are wandering around the battlefield, preparing food and generally attending to our own comforts, me, myself and I.

In a time of War, battles are won by the strategic concentration of force. Soldiers don't just attack along a scattered front. They follow a plan designed by a general with a big map and lots of information. In these Last days we need Divine Strategic Plans that come straight from the Father's heart concerning the Nations.

We must discern the gates of our cities, the strong man and the territorial spirits at work in that certain City, Nation, or Country. A lot of us have lost heart concerning our Future. Your Purpose is to discern the Gates of your City and bind the strong man and plunder his goods.

Why an Army? Because we are at War. Our Enemy is Real, and his Mandate is to destroy Mankind and he is doing a pretty good job of it. Wake up and look around you. Either you're drafted or you're a volunteer Soldier, *"that he may please him who hath chosen him to be a Solider."* In times past many were drafted into the service during the times of War. Others willingly enlisted and chose to battle for their Country. Once they become a part of the service it didn't matter whether they had been drafted or whether they had volunteered. It didn't matter what they were in Civilian life, now they are Soldiers.

The Apostle Paul serves as an example of a good solider. For example: He was stoned, shipwrecked, beaten, and placed in Prison and Dungeons. But when we break a nail or can't pay a bill we are ready to throw in the towel and kick Jesus to the side or murmur that *"this Faith stuff just doesn't work!"* All of these Paul called "Light Afflictions."

CHAPTER FIVE
UNDERSTANDING YOUR VALUE

YOU MATTER

We can't fulfill Gods purpose for our life, if we don't understand our value in God. Lack of value for oneself, is one of the major reasons for depression, sickness, suicide, failure in marriage and even relationships and careers.

Too often, we base our value on how somebody is treating us, how successful we are, or how perfectly we have lived our life. The problem is that all those things can change.

If you're getting your value out of how people treat you, if they hurt or disappoint you, you're going to feel devalued. If you're basing your value on your achievements, how much you make, what kind of car you drive, the title behind your name, then if something happens and you no longer have that position, your business goes down, then your value will go down.

Some people don't feel good about themselves because they've made mistakes in life, they're not where they thought they would be; now they're living insecure, feeling inferior; they're basing their value on their performance.

Your value should be based solely on the fact that you are a child of the highest God; the Creator of the universe breathed His life into you. How someone treats you doesn't change your value; what they say or do doesn't lessen who you are. The mistakes you've made don't decrease your value; that's what you did, not who you are.

You can buy a bigger house, drive a better car, but that doesn't make you any more valuable; that increases your net worth, not your self-worth. You were already valuable when you had a small apartment and no title behind your name; that new position may give you more influence, but not more value.

You can be a stay at home mom raising your children; you may not have the influence of a CEO, but you have the same value.

Value is not based on what you do, what you make, who you know; that's superficial, those things can change. Your value comes from your Creator. God breathed His life into you; you have the DNA of Almighty God and royalty in your blood. But the enemy works overtime trying to devalue us; he'd love for you to go through life letting what people say make you feel inferior, comparing your life to someone else's, thinking that you'll feel good about yourself when you catch up to them, live in that neighborhood, perform perfectly or break that addiction.

Nothing you do, achieve or overcome will make you any more valuable; you are valuable right now. God calls you a masterpiece.

You are one of a kind; you didn't come off an assembly line, mass-produced, God made you unique. Put your shoulders back, start carrying yourself with confidence; you have been fearfully and wonderfully made.

In Luke 4:1-9 and 4:1-5 Jesus was tempted by the Devil, three times trying to make Jesus prove His worth, but Jesus rebuked him and let the devil know that His worth doesn't come from anything the devil was showing Him because the devil was trying to make

Jesus' value be based on His performance; His ability to perform a miracle.

He was saying, in effect, *"I don't have to do anything to prove who I am, or perform to feel good about myself; I know who I Am."* The enemy couldn't deceive Him into basing His value on performance, so He tried to get Him to base His value on possessions:

Jesus was saying, *"I don't need possessions to prove My worth and value. I don't have to have what you think is important to feel good about who I am,"* and when the devil saw that Jesus refused to fall for any of his lies, the enemy (the Devil) tried one final thing, popularity: this is what he said:

> *The devil led Him to Jerusalem and had Him stand on the*
> *highest point of the temple. "If you are the Son of God," he said,*
> *"throw yourself down from here. For it is written:*
> *" 'He will command His angels concerning you*
> *to guard you carefully; they will lift you up in their hands, so*
> *that you will not strike your foot against a stone.' "*
> Luke 4:9-11

The devil was trying to get Jesus to show off; everybody would see and be amazed, He'd gain instant popularity, but Jesus didn't need popularity to know who He was, the Son of the Living God.

The enemy tried to deceive Jesus into proving who He was. A lot of people live in proving mode; they can't feel good about themselves unless they prove to people that they're important and talented.

It's a constant struggle to out-do, out-perform and out-dress; it's very freeing when you realize that you don't have to prove anything or impress people. Take the pressure off. It takes a lot of energy to compete, prove and impress.

If you live in proving mode, it's like you're on a treadmill; as soon as you prove to one person that you're OK, you'll see somebody else that you need to impress, it's a never-ending cycle. Get off the treadmill; you don't have to prove anything.

These days, there's so much emphasis on name brands; sometimes, we have so many other names on us, we don't know our own name. We're counting on all the name brands and outside labels, to make us feel important. There's nothing wrong with owning them, but don't let them be the reason that you feel good about who you are.

The latest thing will soon be outdated; if you live possession-based, you have to keep running from thing to thing and it will wear you out.

Relax; you can't get any more valuable. You can buy more clothes, and get more friends, but that doesn't change your value. Are you trying to prove your worth or value by who you know or what you wear? Or, can you say like Jesus, *"I don't have to have popularity, possessions, or performance to feel good about myself; I am secure in who I am and in who God made me to be?"*

When Jesus was riding into town on Palm Sunday, He received a hero's welcome, but a few days later, those same people crucified

Him and mocked Him, even His closest friends and companions deserted, denied and betrayed Him.

They brought the donkey and the colt and placed their cloaks on them for Jesus to sit on. A very large crowd spread their cloaks on the road, while others cut branches from the trees and spread them on the road. The crowds that went ahead of Him and those that followed shouted, *"Hosanna to the Son of David!"* (Matthew 21:7-9)

> *"What shall I do, then, with Jesus who is called the Messiah?"*
> *Pilate asked. They all answered, "Crucify Him!"*
> Matthew 27:22

When Jesus went to trial, and needed His closest friends to support Him, His disciples, the ones that He had poured His life into, weren't anywhere around.

If you base your value on people's support or how much they approve and encourage you, if they stop doing that, you'll feel devalued. If they tell you that you're great, you'll feel great, but if they change their mind, you won't feel great anymore.

People will say that you're beautiful one day, and not care for you the next. If you don't know who you are without them or if they leave, you'll be lost; your identity was caught up in who they made you to be, and you'll try to find somebody else to tell you who you are.

Let your Heavenly Father tell you who you are; get your value, self-worth and approval from Him. He says that you're a masterpiece, one of a kind and a prized possession. It doesn't matter if somebody criticizes you; they don't determine your value, and they can't change it, so what they say doesn't make you any less a masterpiece.

You don't need their approval, encouragement, or validation; don't give away your power or put your value and identity into somebody else's hands. Even good people can't give you everything you need; somebody that loves you very much cannot keep you approved, validated or feeling secure.

Sometimes, we're putting pressure on people to keep us fixed; let them off the hook, they're not your savior.

People have issues, they don't know any better; messed-up people can mess you up. If you're basing your value on what they give you, you could end up dysfunctional. Don't let messed-up people ruin the rest of your life; if somebody hurt you, there's a tendency to internalize it, and think that there's something wrong with you; no, they're treating you out of their hurts.

Hurting people end up hurting other people; that's the enemy trying to steal your sense of value. If somebody did you wrong, instead of internalizing it, think that maybe they felt so unlovable that they tried to project it on you.

If your parents didn't approve you, don't let that keep you from your destiny. Base your value on what God said about you; that's going to lift you up. The Bible says in Isaiah 49:16, *"See, I have written your name on the Palms of My Hands."*

Do you see that, God is always thinking about you? Don't spend your life trying to get something that people cannot give; let it go, or you'll be frustrated.

David didn't have his father's approval; when the prophet Samuel came to anoint one of Jesse's son's, Jesse didn't even bring David in from the fields. Sometimes, the people closest to you can't see the greatness in you; they discount and dismiss you; don't take it personally, just keep being your best and getting your approval from your Heavenly Father. In John 7:5, Jesus' brothers, the people that should've supported Him the most did not believe in Him.

Beloved, people may leave you out, but God doesn't. If David had to have his family's approval, he would never have taken the throne. Quit trying to make people be for you who they are never going to be for you. If you needed their approval, you would get it; if you're not getting it that means that you don't need it to become who you were meant to be.

Sometimes, it's God teaching us to go to Him and not to people; David's brothers made fun of him, his father discounted him, he was stuck out in the fields, but instead of complaining or feeling inferior, he turned to God. He's the one that wrote: Psalm 27:10 (AMPC)

Although my father and my mother have forsaken me, yet the Lord will take me up [adopt me as His child].

We all have people that are not giving us their approval. Don't live frustrated, trying to convince them to affirm you; let it go and keep your head held high, knowing that you're approved of by your Creator. You may feel average and ordinary, but because of your

Maker, you are extremely valuable. Psalm 139:14 (NIV) says, *"I praise You because I am fearfully and wonderfully made; Your Works are wonderful."*

If you're going to recognize your value, you have to see yourself as wonderful, not because of who you are, but because of who made you and died for you. Life will try to make you feel like you're anything but amazing; disappointments, betrayal and rejection, will try to steal your sense of value.

People may try to make you feel average; do you want to believe what they say about you, or what God says about you? The scripture says in First John 4:4 that you belong to God.

You may feel average, think you look ordinary and that there is nothing special about you, but because of who you belong to, that makes you extremely valuable. Don't let people discount you, or your own thoughts push you down; put your shoulders back, you belong to God!

You don't have to prove anything, try to impress people, just be who you are; be amazing! If you'll do this, every chain that's held you back is being broken; you're going to live free, confident, secure, valuable, and become the masterpiece that God created you to be.

WHERE DO YOU GET YOUR VALUE?

One of the greatest needs we all have is to feel a sense of self-worth. Deep down, we need to know that we're important and that our lives matter. We want to know that we have something great to offer. So often, people base their self-worth on things that don't last like looks, achievements and possessions.

They feel important if they drive the fastest car or own the latest gadget. The problem is that those things can change. When you base your self-worth on temporary things that can change, then your self-worth will change.

Some people find their value in other people. However, if you find your value in how others make you feel and they hurt you or disappoint you, very likely you'll turn it on yourself and think, *"There must be something wrong with me."* No, the only problem is that you're getting your self-worth from the wrong places.

Where should we get our value? Where should we find our self-worth? Our value should come solely from the fact that we are children of the Highest God. We should know that we are important because God says we are important.

Too often, we base our value on how somebody is treating us, how successful we are or how perfectly we have lived our life

---

The value God placed on you is permanent. Nothing you can do, nothing anyone else can do, will ever be able to change that.

I encourage you to check your heart today and make sure you aren't finding your worth in anything other than the love of Christ. Find rest and peace in Him today knowing that your worth is forever established in heaven…the LORD has chosen you to be His Treasured Possession. (Deuteronomy 14:2, NIV)

CHAPTER SIX
DISCOVERING AND FULFILLING PURPOSE

The purpose of your life is far greater than your own personal fulfillment, your peace of mind or even your happiness. It's far greater than your family or your career. Or even your wildest dreams and ambitions. If you want to know why you were placed on this planet, you must begin with God. (Jeremiah 1:5) Placing God in the center of all you do is the first step in knowing your Purpose.

I discovered my Purpose in my own personal life through seeking God first and developing a consistent prayer life. In my teenage years I learned a key principle of making God a Priority in every area of my life, which opened the door to what I do to this very day, working for God full time and being afforded the privilege to take the Gospel of Jesus Christ all over the World. To live a life serving and helping humanity at any cost is my deepest Passion and desire.

The highest form of purpose is a lifestyle of serving others

There has always been a force driving me beyond the comforts of our Western Culture beyond selfish gratifications.

The life that is laid down, is the life that is picked up, which is the life of Christ being seen through your life of service to others. The greatest investment you can make in this life is in the life of Humans. Your life of service to others and not to be bias in who we decide to help or serve with no hidden agendas and motives attached. Just imagine if Jesus had those motives when it came to him going to the Cross to die for the sins of the whole World.

Understanding our identity in Christ gives us purpose. God has a specific purpose for each of us, a unique calling for every individual. Our shared and primary purpose is to become disciples of Jesus Christ. Our secondary callings are unique and birthed out of our submission to the primary calling.

The greatest investment you can make in
this life is in the life of Humans

The body of Christ misses out when we attempt to force all women into one constrained understanding of the role and responsibilities of women.

Christ's transformation does not mean we blindly do as other good and godly people say we should. If we are simply content to go along just to get along, we'll never come to realize our true purpose in life.

A great mentor and a safe community of believers will consistently point us to Christ and challenge us to follow Him as we seek clarity on our faith journeys. A godly mentor models Christ's character, while calling us to completely surrender our will and desires to God's will for our lives.

God is the Creator of all things, and His creative vision is big enough to include women from all walks and stages of life, from different backgrounds, cultures, and generations.

His will is big enough to include young girls like Rhoda, who commit themselves to prayer, and virgins like Mary, the young mother of Jesus. His plans are big enough for women like Elizabeth, Rachel, and Hannah all of whom experienced prolonged seasons of infertility.

His purposes include women with pagan pasts like Ruth, prostitutes like Rahab, and rejected, widowed, or adulterous women like the Samaritan woman at the well.

He sees marginalized and enslaved women like Hagar, and old women like the prophetess Anna. We compassionately embrace women like these because God's purpose and plans include all of them.

Sadly, we live in a world where women constantly receive messages that communicate, *"you' are not valuable."* You're not smart enough for this job or capable enough to earn that amount of income.

You're not skinny enough to fit into those jeans. You're not attractive enough to marry that man or to have a man fully commit to only you. You're not competent enough to be a leader. You're not a great parent. You're not an excellent wife.

And when we are insecure or feel inadequate, it's easy to degrade or reject women who are either more confident than we are or who have made different choices from our own. This rejection somehow makes us feel better about ourselves and more comfortable with our choices, if only for a moment.

Understanding why God put you here is one of the most important principles when it comes to discovering your unique purpose and calling in life. The reason is that knowing why you are here on earth helps you answer the question of why God has uniquely gifted you the way He has, and what He has called you to accomplish individually.

There's nothing more exciting than to discover your purpose, your area of calling and really focus on it! Don't let the enemy tell you you've been forgotten or left out. God has not left anybody out.

You have talents, you have abilities, you have natural strengths and you need to be aware of what they are and make sure that you're taking advantage of them and using them for His glory. There is something important that only you can accomplish for God!

Ever since you were small, someone has been telling you what you can't do. Your mother told you that you couldn't walk down the middle of the street, your father told you that you couldn't ride your bike without reflectors and your teachers told you that you couldn't run in the hallway.

During life, there are hundreds of people who not only tell us what we cannot do, but what we can't accomplish. *"You can't be a chemist. You're not analytical enough." "You can't be a professional singer. You're not attractive enough." "There is no way you'll make it as a teacher. You're not patient enough." "You must be kidding! You want to be a pastor's wife? You won't be a good role model."*

Sadly, we often fear the criticism of others and when it does happen, we take it to heart. For this reason, even into adulthood, we're often waiting for someone to tell us it's OK to "cross the street" to our God-given purpose because we are afraid that if we blow it we'll look like an idiot and then what will they say?

IF GOD BE FOR YOU, WHO CAN BE AGAINST YOU?

Several years ago, I realized I'd been waiting for someone to encourage me to write a book. I thought if another, more successful writer validated me, then I could start moving toward the dream that God had placed in my heart.

Deep down I didn't want to look foolish. One day as I browsed the bookstore for inspiration from an accomplished writer, the Holy Spirit spoke to my heart and said, *"Why are you looking for a leader outside yourself? Write what I have given you."*

No matter who you are, or what you want to accomplish, the only leader you need to move toward your purpose is the Holy Spirit. If God is for you, who can be against you? (Romans 8:31)

Which also begs the question, "Why do we fear criticism?" Even Jesus knew when to ignore naysayers who wanted to prevent Him from accomplishing His purpose.

In Luke 4:30, those in His hometown became furious when He said He was sent by God. To destroy Him, they drove Him out of town to the top of a hill, so they could throw Him over a cliff.

What did Jesus do? He walked through the crowd and went His way. Because He knew who He was and who His Father was, He decided He would "cross the street" to His God-given purpose, even if only God agreed.

Sometimes the best way to move on to God's purpose for us is to ignore negative evaluations and comments and, just like Jesus, go merrily on our way.

God loves you and He has a plan for your life. You are a wonderful creation made by God and you have a unique purpose to fulfill in this world.

Ephesians 2:10 (AMP) says that as Christians, *"We are God's [own] handiwork (His workmanship), recreated in Christ Jesus, [born anew] that we may do those good works which God predestined (planned beforehand) for us [taking paths which He prepared ahead of time], that we should walk in them [living the good life which He prearranged and made ready for us to live]."*

It's so exciting to know we are each created with a purpose and God has a good life that He has prepared in advance for us to live. But it's important to understand that we have an enemy, Satan, who wants to keep us from having the life Jesus died to give us.

Satan has a plan for us, too, and his plan is destruction and death. John 10:10 (AMP) says, *"The enemy comes only to steal and kill and destroy. I came that they may have and enjoy life, and have it in abundance (to the full, till it overflows)."*

The good news is we have everything we need through Christ to overcome the enemy. We just must know who we are in Christ, believe that we have His authority, and know how to release the power God has given us.

THE MEASURE OF YOUR FAITH

Faith in God is required for us to release the power and authority we have in Christ. Romans 12:3 (NASB) says, *"...God has allotted to each a measure of faith."* This means God has given you enough faith to do His Will, whatever it may be and no matter what the enemy throws at you to stop you.

There are many challenges and difficult situations we must face in life. You may have a child with special needs to care for, or maybe you're a single mother or father. You could have a devastating illness or have serious financial problems. Whatever your situation is, God has given you everything you need, through Christ, to keep you moving forward in His plan for your life.

We need to always remember that God is greater than our problems – nothing is too hard for Him and nothing catches Him by surprise.

When we're going through hard times and the enemy is attacking us, we don't need to ask, *"What can I do?"* The question is, "What can God do?" The Word says all things are possible with God, and greater is He who lives in me than he who is in the world. (Matthew 19:26 and First John 4:4.)

I want you to really get this in your heart today: In Christ, you have enough faith and the strength you need to do whatever you need to do in life! (Philippians 4:13.) Get rid of "I can't" thinking and focus on the truth of God's Word, which says, "I can do all things through Christ who strengthens me!"

THE SIMPLE SOLUTION TO OVERCOME THE ENEMIES ATTACK ON YOUR PURPOSE

Prayer is a simple, powerful way to interrupt Satan's plan because we release our faith through prayer. We need to learn to pray our way through the day; First Thessalonians 5:17 (AMP) says, *"Be unceasing in prayer [praying perseveringly]."* We must pray from a Heavenly Perspective. We are not dealing from the Earth Realm.

We are battling in the Heavenly Realms, and your either in or out, there is no room for a soft sport in the supernatural. We have to know that the devil is not playing it safe, he is coming at us every day with all he's got, and we've got to live each day battle ready.

Something happens when men disconnect from the natural and climb up to higher height and dimensions in the spirit. There is a height in prayers that you approach which launches you into supernatural abilities, beyond this natural world. Prayer is contagious, and it releases mighty victories and unprecedented and explosive testimonies.

This basically means prayer can be as natural as breathing, and our first response in every situation. It's so amazing that we can talk to God all the time, in every situation. We are the law enforcement agents for the Kingdom of God. We are putting a divine arrest on the enemy and his camp.

Now the enemy doesn't want us to pray, so he will do everything he can to discourage us. He wants us to think prayer is hard, that we need to use eloquent speech and sound poetic, that we need to be careful what we ask God for, so we don't overload Him with too many requests, or that we have to be in a certain place with a certain posture (on our knees, head bowed, eyes closed) for God to hear us. But it's simple to pray effectively.

> *Prayer is contagious, it releases mighty victories and unprecedented and explosive testimonies*

James 5:16 (AMP) says, *"The earnest (heartfelt, continued) prayer of a righteous man makes tremendous power available [dynamic in its working]."* God wants you to come to Him honestly, with a sincere heart, and just talk to Him as a friend.

Be yourself and don't approach conversation with God as a religious activity. Humble yourself before Him and open your heart to Him. He loves you and wants you to walk in His will for your life victoriously.

As a believer in Jesus Christ, you are God's child and He is with you. He will never leave you nor forsake you. He is the Almighty God, and if God is for you, if He is on your side, who can be against you? In Christ, you have what you need today to live in victory.

All you need to do is believe it and do what God is showing you to do in His Word and as He speaks to your heart. Put your faith in God constantly. Pray, take God-inspired action, and fulfill your true purpose in life!

Can you imagine what Christ's life on earth would have been like if He had been self-protective and feared criticism?

After being mocked by political groups, old and young men and spiteful Pharisees, He would have determined who He would associate with, what He would say in His final hours on earth; and rather than keeping His mouth shut when He was falsely accused, He would have defended Himself.

When His enemies spit in His face, He would have retaliated. When they called Him names, He would have called down a legion of angels to defend Him. When they marched Him to Golgotha, He would have run. And rather than laying down His life to give His all to those He loved, the redemption of humans would have been lost in His misguided passion of self-protection and the fear of criticism.

When we fear criticism and are overly self-protective, we miss out on being a gift to others. You see, your purpose is not just about you; it's about many people that God wants to influence and help through you.

So, if you struggle with criticism and self-protection, get alone with God and ask Him to give you the strength you need to move forward in your purpose in faith. And remember, you are living your life for the approval of just One.

EVEN THE SAINTS EXPERIENCE CRITICISM

Throughout Scripture, men and women who were called to do something significant for God experienced criticism. When Moses led the children of Israel through the desert, he cried out to God many times because those who followed him blamed and criticized him.

Noah's neighbors laughed and mocked him when he built the ark. Paul was labeled as overzealous, unimpressive in person and insincere. Every one of the disciples was criticized and, except for John, all were criticized right to their deaths.

The point is this: If we insist on being comfortable by avoiding the criticism of others, we will not fulfill the purpose that God has for us. Even though comfort and freedom from criticism is on our checklist it's not on God's. His is a higher standard of virtue and redemption.

REMEMBER YOU'RE IN A BATTLE

In his book, "The Believer's Armor," John MacArthur writes, *"You have all the resources, power and principles to live the Christian life. Even though power is available to follow Godly principles, the enemy wants to withstand any good thing that God sets out to do. He will attempt to thwart God's divine purpose for your life."*

As you can see, one of the main ways that Satan wants to thwart your purpose is by causing you to fear criticism. But God wants to provide you with the courage you need to say no to the fear of criticism and yes to Him. Isaiah 53:4 says that Jesus was despised, rejected and not esteemed; so, He knows full well the battle that rages against us with criticism.

The question is this: Will you hold His hand, look the fear of criticism in the eye, step out in faith and live out your God-given purpose for the sake of others and for Christ? He's waiting for you to say yes.

When I once watched paramedics arrive at an accident within minutes, I was in awe of how quickly they had come. What if they didn't have a map? I wondered. Most likely, they would have driven in circles with a next-to-nothing chance of arriving at their destination.

Because goals are the "map" that will guide you toward your God-given purpose, without setting them you will also wander in circles without getting where you need to go.

SETTING GOALS IS NOT UNSPIRITUAL

Many people wrongly think, *"Goal setting is unspiritual because it shows a lack of trust. It's not right to plan. Instead, people should wait for God to lead them."*

Granted, God doesn't want us to forge ahead in pride without consulting Him for direction. But neither does He want us to sit around without acting, because He's given us gifts and talents and has also said that we are called to do good works (Ephesians 2: 8-10, Romans 12:4-8, Matthew 25:14-30).

Forging ahead without seeking God or sitting back and doing nothing can stem from fear or a lack of faith. However, setting goals and consulting with Him shows that you trust Him and believe that He can lead you while you are moving forward.

As you progress in your purpose and God reveals more information to you, keep a dialogue open with Him, pay attention to the road signs He provides along the way and listen to Him speak to you through His Word and the Holy Spirit. Then you can be confident that He will show you when you are in and out of His Will.

SET GOALS IN THE CONTEXT OF THE TOTAL PERSON THAT GOD HAS MADE YOU TO BE

There are many ways to approach goal setting. Some people look at the big picture, then break goals down into smaller chunks, and some like to take a looser approach. However, no matter how you set goals, it's important to consider the total of how God made you in the process.

God created you (and every person on planet Earth) with several parts. Like a pie with separate pieces, each part is critical to who you are; and these parts must be considered when you set goals.

The five parts of a person include:
- Spiritual
- Family
- Social
- Physical
- Work

If you fail to give each part the proper attention and care as you reach toward your God-given purpose, you'll experience problems.

For example, because God created you as a spiritual being, He wants you to love Him with your whole heart, soul and mind (Matthew 22: 37-40). This means that your goals must agree with your spiritual convictions.

If you set goals that go against what you know God asks of you, you will become fragmented emotionally and intellectually and you will lose your joy and enthusiasm.

Additionally, because God also created you to need connection with others, if you neglect the social aspect of your life and become "all work and no play" you will become out of balance and you'll most likely experience physical, emotional, social and spiritual troubles.

There's no doubt that God wants you to fulfill your purpose. In fact, it's your duty since He has given you gifts to do so. However, be mindful not to neglect any of the five areas that make up who you are while you do His work.

Finally, remember that the world does not rest on your shoulders. You will make mistakes in setting goals. It's OK. Because God wants to see you do His will, He will teach you the way to go as you walk in faith (Psalm 32:8).

CHAPTER SEVEN
SPEAKING THE BLESSINGS OVER YOUR LIFE

Have you thought about how the people in your life need your blessing? They need your approval. They need to hear you say, "I'm proud of you. You're going to do great things." That's speaking the blessing.

Nothing determines your Destiny like your words. I have been so blessed to have they the world greatest Apostles and Pastors in the World in Tony and Cynthia Brazelton. The greatest thing they taught me was the power of confession and Faith. Like Apostle Cynthia Brazelton always says, *"It is what you say it is."* God has given us the power to frame and create the world that we want to see for our lives, children, Nation etc. Blessing is life giving and has creative power. I feel strongly that speaking and declaring blessings is on the Father's agenda right now.

The first words God spoke over Adam and Eve were words of blessing (Genesis 1:27-29) and the last words Jesus spoke over the assembled Group of disciples as He was ascending to Heaven were word of blessing (Luke 24:50-52). Jesus taught His followers to bless, and he continually demonstrated it.

The World around us views blessing as an occasional happy event. However, the truth is, that in Christ you are already blessed and will always be. (Ephesians1:3) Jesus is the source of your personal blessing and through Him you have the ability to bless others. When you bless in accordance with the Father's intent and purpose, your blessing is Prophetic and you will see complete fulfillment and manifestation every time.

The Father speaks His word of blessing ahead of time, speaking forward, and that blessing has the power to bring His intention to pass. In our culture today, people are more likely to complain, speak negatively and criticize, than to bless.

People are more likely to forecast harm than prophecy good. Because of this, speaking and praying words of blessing may seem unnatural for us at first. However, it is time to align our words and our lifestyle with the Kingdom of God. This teaches us something about kingdom culture.

You too have the ability to bless, and to release the Shalom of God, something tangible imparted by the Holy Spirit. Your words will be full of power; your very words hold weight. Blessing is powerful to cut through the plans and strategies of the enemy. Life-giving words, sourced from the Father's heart, break the power of cursing and negativity (Proverbs 18:21). Blessing flows out of an Abundance mindset, the Kingdom mindset is one of plenty and abundance.

When you say to the people you love, "I'm so glad you're in my life. You mean the world to me," you just gave them a blessing. When you tell one of your employees, coworkers or a student, "You amaze me with your ability. You have such a bright future," those are not just nice compliments. When you speak the blessing, you're releasing God's wisdom, protection, favor and abundance into their hearts. You can literally help shape their destiny. One word of encouragement, one word of approval can be what helps someone step up to who God created them to be.

Today, choose to speak the blessing. Sow good seeds into the lives of the people you love. Remember, what you make happen for others, God will make happen for you. Sow blessing and reap blessing and experience His favor all the days of your life!

USE YOUR WORDS TO SHAPE YOUR FUTURE

Words have power. They can hurt, and they can bless. But the power of words reaches much further than the impact they make on our emotions. Our words have supernatural power that changes circumstances and shapes destinies. In fact, it is our unique ability to choose and speak words that distinguishes man from the rest of God's creation.

Change Your Words, Change Your World, Shape Your Future

Man is created in God's image and it was not just thoughts but words that God used to create us and the universe in which we live. When He said, *"Light be,"* light was. Words are the way God works.

Hebrews 11:3 describes this operating principle of creation this way: *"Through faith we understand that the worlds were framed by the word of God, so that things which are seen were not made of things which do appear."* Words are spiritual; they carry power. Proverbs 12:14 tells us that we shall be satisfied with good by the fruit of our mouths.

This process begins with salvation. The lost man does this when he declares Jesus Lord of his life: *"The word is nigh thee, even in thy mouth, and in thy heart: that is, the word of faith, which we preach; that if thou shalt confess with thy mouth the Lord Jesus, and shalt believe in thine heart that God hath raised him from the dead, thou shalt be saved. For with the heart man believeth unto righteousness; and with the mouth confession is made unto salvation."* (Romans 10:8-10)

Confession is not denying physical facts and temporary circumstances. It is declaring what God, who never changes, has said about the outcome and standing in faith until all temporary conditions line up with His eternal declaration.

Confession is a vital part of our spiritual growth as a believer. Jesus indicated this in describing the importance of speaking His Father's words and not His own: *"I do nothing of myself; but as my Father hath taught me, I speak these things. If ye continue in my word, then are ye my disciples indeed."* (John 8:28, 31)

In answering the question how He would manifest Himself to His disciples after His resurrection, Jesus replied: *"If a man loves me, he will keep My words: and My Father will love him, and we will come unto him, and make our abode with him. ...The word which ye hear is not Mine, but the Father's which sent me."* (John 14:23-24)

Israel's King David understood this. He brought his soul—his mind, will and emotions—in line with God's Word by speaking to it: *"Bless the Lord, O my soul: and all that is within me, bless his holy name. Bless the Lord, O my soul, and forget not all his benefits."* (Psalm 103:1-2)

Confession of the Word of God isn't lying.

We are not trying to get God to do anything. Those benefits Gods have given us in His Word are ours already and Satan is trying to steal them! The process of believing and speaking is what brings every benefit of our salvation promised in God's Word from heaven into our lives.

To tell someone you are healed because the Bible says *"by His stripes you were healed"* is speaking the truth. Jesus has already redeemed you from the curse of the law. (Deuteronomy 28; Galatians 3:13)

Words reveal what we truly believe. Jesus said, *"Out of the abundance of the heart the mouth speaks. By thy words thou shalt be justified, and by thy words thou shalt be condemned."* (Matthew 12:34, 37) That is why it is so important to say what God has said. Do this, not so others can hear you, but so your soul will receive instruction on what to believe and agree with instead of the symptoms in your body, situations in your life and fear-based thinking and talking what you hear from others around you.

How do we give glory to God? By honoring the words, He has spoken and demonstrating our trust in Him. Our first step of acting on our faith in His Word is to agree with and say the thing He has said.

Keeping Jesus' words means more than just doing what He said. It also means living as He lived. He lived never saying or doing anything He did not first hear the Father say or see the Father do.

As His disciples, our words should be in complete agreement with what the Father has spoken concerning us. When we speak His words in faith, they have the same power to change our circumstances as when He spoke Creation into being.

Jesus' ministry to us today includes His position as High Priest of our profession, or confession. (Hebrews 3:1) To profess means to "say the same thing." When we say only what God has said, His words have the same power spoken in faith out of our lips as they did when He originally spoke them.

Jesus, as our High Priest, makes sure those words the Father has spoken come to pass in our lives. That is why we are instructed in Hebrews to *"hold fast the profession [confession] of our faith without wavering; (for he is faithful that promised)."* (10:23; 4:14)

It's true that things may not change soon. On the other hand, it's also true that God is bigger than any situation. The question is, on which side will we put our faith? If I pray for someone to be healed but speak as though they never will be, what does that say about my faith? What does it say about my confidence in the power of God? If I truly believe that my Lord can do anything, then my speech should back up that belief. I should speak positive words of faith.

If I'm looking for a job in a tough economy, instead of telling myself, *"Man, no one is hiring,"* I could say, *"Thank you Jesus for the doors you're opening and for the opportunities you're leading me to!"* Yes, that can be easier said than done. But does God take notice of our faith and attitude? Have a look...

But without faith it is impossible to please Him: for he that cometh to God must believe that He is, and that He is a rewarder of them that diligently seek Him.
Hebrews 11:6

By speaking life, I don't mean we should just spout empty words to sound like we have faith. Faith is something we get by the Word of God and experience.

A politician we know of ran on a platform of "Hope and Change." He didn't have much experience, nor did he have any specifics about what "Hope and Change" meant, but regardless, he won his campaign. Before long however, his inexperience caught up to him, and his words have fallen flat. Without real world experience and a track record of accomplishment, words are just words. The phrase, "Hope and Change" is a joke today.

By contrast, a young shepherd boy told a king he could defeat a giant and bring victory to his people. It sounded pretty farfetched. A shepherd in his youth going up against a giant who's been a warrior from his youth. Are you kidding? But keep reading...

And David said unto Saul, thy servant kept his father's sheep, and there came a lion, and a bear, and took a lamb out of the flock: And I went out after him, and smote him, and delivered it out of his mouth: and when he arose against me, I caught him by his beard, and smote him, and slew him. Thy servant slew both the lion and

the bear: and this uncircumcised Philistine shall be as one of them,
seeing he hath defied the armies of the living God.
First Samuel 17:34-36

David's hope was founded on his past experiences with God. He spoke life and faith to this challenge because he knew his God was able. It's good to remind ourselves of our past victories and encourage ourselves in our God! We should speak life and positive words of faith because our God is Mighty! He is Powerful! He is able to do exceeding abundantly above all that we ask or think, according to the power that worked in us! His word is true, and his track record is stunning.

If speaking positive words of faith is difficult, read Psalm 34 (KJV) out loud, once a day for the rest of the month. Let's brag about our God and remind ourselves of past victories, and even greater ones to come!

IT'S TIME TO USE OUR WORDS TO DECLARE GOOD THINGS

I once read an article about doctors who incorporated "talk therapy" to treat patients suffering with depression. Instead of medicating the problem, the doctors instructed the patients to start making positive declarations over their lives, saying such things as: *"I have a bright future. People like to be around me. Good things are in store."*

Some of the patients were depressed because they were facing life-threatening diseases and felt there was no hope. The doctor asked them, "Has anyone ever survived this disease?" The answers were always yes. So, he told them, "Then I want you to start saying,

'I will make it. I will be one of the people who beats the odds.' Those patients obeyed the doctor's orders, and amazingly, many of them not only came out of their depression, but they also made full recoveries!

It's time to use our words to declare good things! Speak blessings over your life and your family. Throughout the day, say things such as, *"I have the favor of God. I am strong and healthy. I'm well able to do what I need to do."*

Did you know that what you say about yourself has greater impact on you than anything anybody else says about you? Many people are overly critical of themselves, saying, *"I'm so clumsy. I can't do anything right." "I'm so overweight. I'll never get back into shape." "I never get any good breaks."*

They may not realize it, but they are cursing their future. Those words sink into their minds. Before long, they develop a defeated mentality, low self-esteem and diminished confidence. Worse yet, those negative mindsets can interfere with God's plan for their lives.

One of the best ways to break free from such strongholds is simply by speaking words of victory. Every day look in the mirror and declare, *"God's Word says I am strong. God is fighting my battles for me. I'm excited about my future."*

Maybe you are lonely because you don't have a lot of friends. Instead of complaining, start declaring, *"God is bringing great people into my life. I know He loves me, so I can risk loving others."*

Speak blessings over your life, and as you do, you'll go out with more confidence, you'll be more congenial, and in turn, you will attract new friends. When discouragement comes, instead of sitting back and accepting it, say, *"No, I'm a victor and not a victim. I may have been defeated before, but the past is the past. This is a new day."*

It's not enough just to think it; you need to hear it, because what we constantly hear ourselves saying we will eventually believe. Some people live in a perpetual state of financial crisis. They can't seem to pay their bills always living "under their circumstances" and constantly speaking defeat. If you are struggling financially, remind yourself repeatedly, *"I am the head and I am not the tail. I will lend, and I will not borrow. Everything I touch will prosper and succeed."*

"Oh, Keshia, I can't say that," you may be thinking. *"None of that is true in my life."* Yes, it is true! That is what faith is all about. The world says you need to see it to believe it, but God says you must believe and then you'll see it. You must speak it by faith.

Make a list of your goals, your dreams, the areas where you want to see change. Confirm your desires by Scripture, and then every day before you leave the house, speak those blessings aloud. Something supernatural happens when you speak those words aloud.

Maybe you struggle with condemnation because of past mistakes. Each day, boldly declare, *"I am the righteousness of God in Christ Jesus. God is pleased with me. He is on my side."*

If you say something like that on a consistent basis, guilt and condemnation won't hang around. Find the Scriptures that apply to your situation and then declare them. This is especially important in areas in which you continually struggle.

Do not let another critical word come out of your mouth about yourself. Instead, take a few minutes every day to bless your life, to declare the victory.

Understand, it's not enough to avoid saying anything negative; you must go on the offensive and start making positive declarations over your life. Remember, your own words will have more impact on your future than anything anybody else says about you.

Friend, if you'll do your part and speak words of victory, God will pour out His favor in exciting, fresh ways in your life, and you will live the abundant life He has in store for you.

YOUR MISTAKES DON'T CANCEL YOUR DESTINY

Back in Bible days, if you would have asked Jacob *"Who are you?"* he would have said, *"I'm a cheater. I'm a deceiver. I'm a liar."* But really, that's not who he was, that's what he did. We've all done things we're not proud of. We've all made mistakes and said things we didn't mean. But because of the blood of Jesus, God isn't holding that against us.

When we repent, scripture says He takes our sin and casts it as far as the east is from the west and remembers it no more. Always remember, God looks beyond your behavior, beyond your

74

performance, and He sees you for who you really are: a person of destiny created in His image with a purpose to fulfill.

If we are going to be all God has called us to be, we must separate our "doing" from our "being". If you live in guilt and condemnation, it will keep you from receiving the mercy and blessings of God. It will limit your life.

That's why it's so important to shake off the past and say, *"No, I am not what I did. I may have failed at my marriage, but I am not a failure." "I may be struggling with alcohol, but I am not an alcoholic. I'm a child of Almighty God, and I know my destiny is bigger than my mistakes. I can do all things through Christ who gives me strength and I will overcome!"*

I think about Moses. As a young man, he had a big dream in his heart. He knew God had called him to help deliver the people of Israel. He started off great. He was passionate and enthusiastic. But one day, he saw someone mistreating one of the Israelites.

And in his zeal to fulfill his purpose, he went over and killed that man. He made a mistake. His heart was right, but his actions were not right.

Someone saw him, and he had to run for his life. He ended up spending forty years on the back side of the desert. He went through a detour. He missed Plan A, but the good news is that God had Plan B. God didn't say, *"Too bad, Moses. You blew it. You had your chance."* No, and He's not saying that to you, either! If you will stay in faith, your destiny will supersede those poor choices.

Forty years later, when God was ready for someone to deliver His people, He didn't go find a younger man. God didn't go find someone who had never made mistakes, someone with a perfect record. He went right back to Moses and said, *"Hey, Moses, I haven't forgotten about you. That mistake didn't cancel your destiny. I'm ready for you now. It's your time. Go out and deliver My people."*

Today, you may have made mistakes or missed good opportunities. It looks like the dream has died or the promise will never come to pass. But God is saying, *"Get ready. Just as I did for Moses, I'm about to open a new door. I'm about to unleash My favor. That setback that was meant to destroy you is a setup for a comeback. That failure that's clouded your future is not the end."* It's a new day, so rise and move forward into the victory God has prepared for you!

YOU ARE A SPIRITUAL BROADCASTING STATION

We are all broadcasting stations, whether we know it or not. Your thoughts, feelings, emotions, faith and fears tend to shape your personal environment. You are constantly sending, receiving and creating your own reality.

Have you ever walked into a room and could sense that something was wrong? I guarantee you that there had been some negative thinking or believing happening in that room before you entered it. We are all surrounded by our own mental atmosphere, which consists of what you have been continually thinking, feeling and believing. A person who is filled with anger, resentment and fear tunes in and picks up vibrations of failure.

Conversely, a person whose thoughts are filled with ideas of success will tune into the successful thoughts around him or her. The thoughts of faith, optimism and happy expectancy.

Today, decide to begin to think on the affirmative side of life. As the song lyrics go, *"accentuate the positive, eliminate the negative."* In doing so, you have decided to send out and receive only positive manifestations in your life.

Tune your mind into the divine mind of God. Know that you draw into your own soul the essence of everything that is good, true and beautiful. Realize the divine presence and the power of God until your whole being responds. Broadcast love, healing and peace to the whole world and it will return to you.

How do you begin to change what we are sending out?

- Be grateful for what you have now, and for what you expect to happen.
- Deliberately tune into the divine mind of God, daily.
- Expect only good to show up in your life.
- Stay away from negative thinking people.
- Monitor the time that you watch or read negative information.

Keep your thoughts and emotions only on what you desire to manifest in your life.

CHAPTER EIGHT
YOU HAVE BEEN CHOSEN FOR THE TIMES

We have entered into an Unprecedented time and Season. None like we have ever seen in this lifetime. You are living in the greatest time ever in Human History, and to think and know You Have Been Chosen for The Times!

You are the very expression of God in the Earth Realm and He is about to exercise His power and authority through your life like never before. The Lord is raising up the remnant of this generation. We are to be as cities on a hill that would draw in all men.

I have seen people becoming cities; lighting up by not allowing our light or love to be restrained or contained. I see each person as a city, a center of trade and distribution; a whole world within themselves yet connected to each other.

They are key people the Lord is raising up for the Times. Such power, authority, and ability rests within each one, yet they are a piece in this movement. They are meant to unify and raise up others. I see each person possessing such a Divine Inspiration of wisdom, insight, and understanding. We are rising up as the Sons of God. The Lord spoke to me personally saying to me there is an Arising and an Uprising in our time. All we are seeing happening around the world, the turbulence, economic meltdown, trade wars, suicide bombings, political and social unrest and marital decay are all uprisings trying to diminish the Arising. But it can't because Gods Glory is overshadowing the uprising.

God is moving with Revival power all through the earth, and we are the ones who are alive in such a remarkable time in all of history. These are merely the birth pangs. God is on the move and we must get ready for all that is about to enter our radar screen.

We can easily get depressed and discouraged at all the difficulties and inconveniences of living in such days as these, but do we realize what a great privilege it is to be alive in this Unprecedented time. It is no accident that we find ourselves here in our day. This is what He has appointed for us.

We could have been favored to live in Reformation times, Puritan times, during the 18th Century Awakenings, in the Civil Rights Movement era or in better times more recently. However, the Lord has chosen us for NOW! We must accept that calling, for we have *"come to the kingdom for such a time as this."* (Esther 4:14)

We have been chosen as a generation of Breakers. Many have gone before us with this Breaker Anointing. The true anointing that upsets that apple cart of religion, that disturbs the peace of complacency, that tears down strongholds in order to rebuild ruined cities that has devastated Generations. We have been chosen to walk in the power of the third generation. We know the story of how Elijah transferred his mantle to Elisha. In accordance with the transferring of the mantle Elisha received a double portion of the anointing.

The power of the third generation is that, according to the math of GOD, the double portion doesn't transfer in another double portion but in exponential increase. We have been called to inherit the dormant mantles and walk in the exponential anointing

I pray that by now you understand how special you are. When you understand that our Father in Heaven is very selective in who He chooses, then will you understand how loved and powerful you are.

The Eternal God desires that those who are called out of this world be His chosen ones as well.

Abba Father is saying children you are in the Fullness of time, a time of Acceleration and Advancement. This is your Season of Wow! This is your season of Testimonies according to Psalms 2:8, and that shall be your portion.

I have given you the Nations as your Inheritance and the entire Earth will belong to you! God's blessings follow you and wait for you at every turn. This is the day of divine doors being open for you and Divine Handshakes! Your Destiny Helpers are in your midst. There is a Rising Up and a going Forth!

Also, I am baptizing you with Fresh Fire for the Hour. You are in the hour of the outpouring of HIS Spirit upon all Flesh! The heavy Weight of His Glory is being released. You have come into full Reality that you are Purpose and as Jesus is, so you are in this World! We are living in Jubilee with the Holy Spirit in this age.

Joel 2:28-29 says, *"Then in those days I will pour My Spirit to all Humanity; Your children will bodily and prophetically speak the Word of God. Your Elders will dream dreams, your young warriors will see visions. No one will be left out. In those days I will offer My Spirit to all servants, both male and female."*

Time as we know it has been swallowed up; The time clock has crashed and we have moved from Chronos time to Kairos time.

CHRONOS TIME

Chronos refers to minutes and seconds. It refers to time as a measurable resource. We tend to think of our time in a Chronos mindset. We think of having 24 hours in a day. We define our work weeks by the number of hours that we work. We have a list of things to do and only so much time to get everything done.

Being conscious of our minutes and seconds is a good thing. We should number our days as the scripture says. Our time on earth is so brief, and we want to be good stewards of every second that we have, to glorify God on this earth.

But ironically, this Chronos mindset can make us miss what Paul is saying in Ephesians 5. Paul instructs us to redeem the Kairos – to pay attention and take advantage of the opportune times and seasons.

KAIROS TIME

Kairos is the word used for time in Ephesians 5:16. Kairos means an appointed time, an opportune moment, or a due season. We only have such a brief opportunity to shepherd our kids when they're still young children. When a friend is experiencing pain, we have a brief window of time in which to reach out to them.

This requires us to make a mental shift. Instead of looking at our time as grains of sand slipping through an hourglass, we view our time as opportunities flying by. Instead of viewing our time as seconds ticking by, we realize that not every second holds the same worth. We are in a Jubilee Season - a Double Jubilee Season.

Time as we know has taken the Passenger seat and Eternity has taken the Driver's Seat and it is moving us into places and Dimensional Realms beyond what we have ever seen in our Present Time. Welcome to the Season of Enlargement!

You have been Chosen for the Times, you are the Catalyst and the Conduits that will carry out the Father's end time agenda in full Partnership with Him. There is a relentless call from God from Heaven to you and what will be your response?

You have been Chosen to awaken the sleeping Giants of this Generation and Time. You have been chosen and called to the duty of surrender of self to the service of God and Man. This Elijah Revolution will change the landscape of Society; everyone will have to make at least some kind of adjustment. This Chosen Generation are the Prophetic Voices of our day. The Spirit of this Age wants you to be silent. But you are the Announcers of Truth Which Is the Gospel of our Lord and King Jesus Christ.

You have been Summoned by the Ancient of Days, the God of the Heavens! The Lord has given the Nations to us as an Inheritance, a gift. We are accountable for the Nations. God chose us for this End Time intervention. You have to become one with the Eternal (Eternity) to make a mark in the Natural Realm. There are so many things unfolding before our very eyes.

Mary was a simple Village girl when she was Chosen for The Times by God to be the vehicle of the Savior of the whole World, coming to the Earth to deliver Mankind from their Sins. There are new rules of engagement in the end times. We have been Chosen for the Times. This Generation will not take a "NO" for an answer. This Generation deserves an awakening and a mighty Outpouring of the Spirit, because "These Are the Days!"

We are living in a Divine Time

There are specific Gates that are tied to the Nations of the Earth (You are a Gate, and a Bridge). The very fragment of our Nation will be impacted by these End Time Warriors. We have been Chosen to Validate this Generation.

You have been called to the Kingdom for the greatest Time in Human History! You could have been in any Dispensation, but you were hand-picked especially for HIS DIVINE Purpose for this Divine Time! He operates outside of Natural Time, which creates the Life of the Overflow where there are no limits and no boundaries.

FULFILLED PROPHECY

At a very tender age, I struggled with a mandate I hadn't quite figured out. My young mind was mesmerized. My disposition and mannerisms were in sharp contrast with those of the other kids and I didn't know why. I was being controlled by something bigger than me, and I had great difficulty handling it. As I grew in age and stature, the eventual manifestation of God's call upon my life became even more bold and relentless.

On so many occasions, I would walk into a place and a *"Man of God"* would look me straight in the eyes and say, *"you are a Woman of God!"* *"You are a Prophetess"*, etc. And all these things were happening at a time when nothing about me on the outside portrayed their declarations.

These declarations all served as confirmations to the numerous often confusing pointers that I have been exposed to, since a teenager. As much as I tried repeatedly to brush it aside, thinking it was mere hallucination, the manifestation continued to grow exponentially. Today I am an International Evangelist who has taken the gospel across the globe.

Today, when I look back on those days of turbulence and confusion, I can only see how faithful and sure God's words and call upon my life remain, even in the face of the most confusing and distractive situations.

Being called to the nations from my mother's womb has placed me in prime of place in the scheme of God's end time program. It is such an honor to be chosen and even more, to serve the purpose of God's kingdom in such a time as this.

"While you were on the floor crying and praying, I saw a sword flamed. I heard "fire of my love", I saw the sword pierce your heart and then it began to be twisted from side to side as if it was tearing your heart to pieces from the inside, then the sword was pulled out of your body with the chopped off heart on it. I then believe God gave you a new heart for your assignment. I was then reminded of something my father said to me, miracles come from broken lives. I believed God was breaking your heart and giving

you a new one to go along with what God is calling you to do. It
reminded me of how my father said God gave him heart to pastor
and that God will give you a heart of love for the call on your life."
(The above is a recorded prophecy spoken to me by my sister in
the lord Minister Antoinette Brazelton in 2010 while on a mission
trip to India.)

There are numerous of such prophecies upon my life from
different servants of God and they are all gradually coming to
fulfillment in my life every day. And the reason why I have chosen
to share this particular prophecy is because I am currently today
walking in it. Today am the founder and president of Love-Aflame
International, an NGO that has been touching lives in Africa and
Asia. So, the same God that fulfilled His spoken word over my life
is the same that will fulfill the prophetic word and promises over
your life. Prophecies work and come to pass. Just believe. It will
tarry but it will surely come to pass. You may not look like it now,
but you are it, in the spiritual.

This truth does not only apply to me. The scriptures declare in
Acts 10:34 that *"God is no respecter of persons."* This simply
means that what is true for my life, and my "yes", is also true for
your life, and your yes.

God will make sure that every detail of your life points you to a
specific end that He has chosen for you.

He literally took my single Yes and multiplied it with so many
adventures and testimonies of His goodness and favor affording me
to travel the world interacting with people of all nations, that has
impacted my life to the very core of my existence.

God will arrange people, places, and things to point you in a direction that He has specifically chosen for your life. If you will take the time to look back and recall special moments and times that had a deep impact on your life. Those very moments were designed to direct you to the place where you are today.

Every aspect of your life is the fulfillment of a Rhema word from God for your life. That does not mean that you will not face life challenges and storms. It simply means because You have been Chosen for the Times, all things are working for your good and you end up where God has intended you to be. When you say yes to God. God begins to unfold an eternity of thoughts. His eternal plan for your life. When you say yes to God, God Himself sees to it that every step that you take under the influence of that sincere Yes is fulfilling something He has said about you before time ever began.

Your life literally becomes a fulfillment of His prophesy. And this is what makes our lives Supernatural, fun and fulfilling. In walking in your sincere Yes to God, you begin to discover what was on the mind of God concerning your life. Nothing about your life is coincidence. Your life and steps has been ordained and commanded by the almighty God.

TODAY YOUR JOURNEY BEGINS

Beloved, you are a chosen one. Take courage and know that He who began an excellent work in you, has already completed it. From this day forward, I declare over you that you will accomplish and complete every assignment that the Father has spoken over your life. Know that with your assignment there will always be trials for you to face and overcome. But you can live with a sense of peace knowing that every step you take has God's word supporting it.

God is setting you apart to be used by Him, there is a price on your life. You are not ordinary or natural. You are an extraordinary person with a lot of deposits of the supernatural on the inside. You literally carry generations inside of you and you are an embodiment of transformation.

Your Heavenly Father, God, has deposited Himself inside of you and the devil knows this, that is why he will continue to throw stones at you in the form of challenges. But the Bible says in John 16:33, *"I have told you these things, so that in me you may have peace. In this world you will have trouble. But take heart! I have overcome the world."*

God is speaking to you every day, through His Word, through a pastor on the radio or TV, and now He is speaking through this book. He is saying son/daughter I have chosen you, I am setting you apart, I have a great destiny ahead for you. Can you hear Him? Those prophecies you keep getting from people, those specific words of revelation you get, those amazing night vision and dreams, those words of strength from your parents and loved ones telling you that there is greatness inside of you, that is God speaking through them.

God is pouring out His Spirit upon this generation, there is a supernatural invasion of the sons of God, but only those who are spiritually positioned will receive this outpouring. You have to awaken spiritually to what God is about to do in this present time.

Everything you have experienced and are experiencing right now, is God trying to take you to where He wants you to be. Those mistakes, those failures, betrayals and rejection, are all working to your advantage. So, the question is what are you going to do about this knowledge? Are you going to allow God to use you? Are you going to allow Him to unveil to you the essence of you being created and why He has chosen you, or are you just going to live a life of purposelessness and mere existence?

This is an Awakening!

ACKNOWLEDGEMENTS

Through the course of this project, I have had the honor of working with numerous amazing people whose ideas, words of encouragement and support towards the completion of this cannot be overemphasized. First of all, I would like to acknowledge my spiritual parents and pastors, Apostle Tony and Cynthia Brazelton, for their timeless leadership over my life and family. I have been blessed with the best Pastors in the world!

Secondly, I would especially like to thank my friend and partner, Pastor Great Igwe for his extensive help throughout the course of this book. Thank you to my friend and partner, Joseph Chidde Okechukwu, for the ideas he gave me and doing parts of the editing for the book. I want to thank my donors and financial partners for all their financial support. I want to thank my core DO LIFE sisters for all your love and support in everything I do in life, you know who you are. I love you all immensely!

Thirdly, I would like to appreciate all my partners, too numerous to mention. Specifically, I'd like to thank LaKesha Williams of Vision to Fruition, Len and Latia Graham of Agara Design Company, for the book cover and Trey Copelin of Tarry Hearken Solutions.

Lastly, I would like to appreciate my son, Isaiah, for his love and sacrifice of always sharing me with the world. Isaiah, you will be great, and you will make a mark in your generation! I would like to thank my mom and dad, sisters and brothers, and nieces and nephews, for your continual, unselfish love and care. Thank you all for helping me fulfill this project and vision. God bless you all!

ABOUT THE AUTHOR

Evangelist Keshia R. Freeland
"Transforming the World, One Heart at A Time"

Evangelist Keshia R. Freeland is a servant called to evangelize the nations through the spreading of hope, compassion and goodwill. She has a unique approach to ministry, which identifies with people of all cultures and meets them wherever they are in life.

Her purpose in ministry is founded upon the scripture: Isaiah 61:1, *"The Spirit of the Lord God is upon me; Because He has anointed me to preach good tidings to the poor. He has sent me to heal the brokenhearted." With a unique love for God's word and a passion for transformation in the lives of His people, she has been sent to minister good tidings: "To help others progress through their circumstances and fulfill God's unique plan and destiny for their lives."*

Keshia serves faithfully at her home church, Victory Christian Ministries International, under the headship of Apostles Tony and Cynthia Brazelton. The mentorship of these Spiritual Parents has caused dynamic acceleration in her growth.

Her stewardship has been proven in multiple offices, which include Deacon, Missionary, Director of Out-Reach and Director of Singles Ministry. Accepting her call into the ministry as a young teenager, she has served successfully and effectively for more than 20 years and has become an internationally known conference speaker.

She has had the liberty to travel locally and abroad - impacting cultures across North America, South America, Africa, Asia, Europe, Mexico and the Caribbean Islands. Evangelist Freeland is the Founder & President of "LoveAflame" International {Pronounced Love-a-Flame}, a Global Response & Charitable Organization, committed to the creation of sustainable welfare for all of mankind with a special emphasis on women and children.

Evangelist Freeland holds a Bachelor of Science degree in Biblical Studies from Lancaster Bible College. She also holds an Honorary Doctor of Divinity degree awarded through more than a decade of traveling the world and transforming communities (internationally) through successful fulfillment of the great commission (Matthew 28: 16-20).

Keshia Freeland
www.keshiafreeland.com

Made in the USA
Columbia, SC
25 June 2018